A RUSSIAN MARTYR

IVAN VASILYEVICH MOISEYEV

Translated by H. K. Neerskov

Edited by John B. Calhoun

Published by
CHRIST FOR THE NATIONS
Dallas, Texas
Litho U.S.A.
Reprinted 1974

Contents

Editor's Note

The following account of the martyrdom of Ivan Vasilyevich Moiseyev was taken from material recently smuggled out of the Soviet Union by a Christian underground organization, working in cooperation with the Danish European Mission in Soborg, Denmark.

The material itself consisted of a tape recording by Moiseyev, his letters, and supporting documentation by his parents and members of an evangelical church group in his home district. Because much of it was recorded ad hoc and under duress, it is somewhat fragmentary and tends to show some confusion on minor details such as names, places and military ranks. Where these discrepancies existed, the editorial policy was to choose the most likely alternative according to the overall context of the story. In the case of unresolvable conflicts, the particular detail was omitted. In neither case was anything of substance lost.

Its literary shortcomings, which the translator has noted in the preface, were obvious from the beginning. The editor, like the translator, faced the choice of either working the English rendition out into a smooth, consistent style or preserving its simple, often choppy but generally straightforward character. The latter alternative was chosen for reasons which it is hoped will be obvious upon reading: there is in the midst of its imperfections a certain manner of expression which magically seems to convey the sense of poignancy and resignation of the simple peasant people who populate so much of the Russian motherland and who are the characters of this story.

Few liberties, therefore, were taken with the text. Only where its literary defects produced real obscurity or confusion were adjustments made, and then only minor ones. As in the case of the few factual discrepancies, nothing of any substance was lost.

As far as the narrative sections are concerned, they were inserted only where necessary to smooth the transition from one part of the material to another, to highlight a particular point in a section, or to give essential background information, as in the introduction or the footnotes. It is felt that the people of the story tell it more eloquently than any narration could ever hope to.

It is to them and the memory of their beloved Ivan that this booklet is affectionately dedicated.

J.B.C.

Dallas, Texas
January 1974

Preface

This booklet contains the true story of a modern martyr, whose life is outstanding because of his tremendous endurance and spiritual courage. It is even more remarkable because, as a result of his steadfastness in the faith, he received spiritual revelations unprecedented in modern times.

It also has a message to us Christians in the Western world who spend so much time fighting over trifles and in theological hair-splitting. We live in a generation which has seen more martyrs than any other. Do we notice? Do we remember them? Do we pray for them?

As will be clear from reading it, this story has not been written by an experienced writer, but by simple Russian believers. In translating it, we have felt obliged to preserve their simple way of expressing things. For this reason it may have certain literary shortcomings.

H. K. Neerskov

Soborg, Denmark
December 1972

CHAPTER 1

Introduction

Ivan Vasilyevich Moiseyev was born in 1952 in the city of Volontirovka, Suvorov District, Moldavian SSR[1]. His father, Vasily Timofeyevich and his mother, Ionna Konstantinova, had eight children (seven sons and a daughter, all of whom were brought up according to the teachings of Jesus Christ, and most of whom eventually consecrated their lives to the Lord's service.

After finishing school in 1968, Ivan came to Christ in the Evangelical Christian Baptist (ECB)[2] Church in Slabodeyska and a year-and-a-half later, in 1970, made a covenant with the Lord by being baptised and becoming a member of the Church. After having been born again he experienced a tremendous desire to witness for Christ. During the few months before he was drafted, he preached the Gospel wtih great enthusiasm and joy both in the Church and to the young people of Volontirovka, where he worked as a delivery driver.

In November 1970 he was drafted into the Soviet Army. Almost from the beginning, he experienced hardships and trials because of his faith. Eventually, because of his steadfast refusal to disavow his beliefs and the all-too-obvious workings of God in his life, he was subjected to severe persecutions and torture. Finally, on July 16, 1972, at the age of twenty, he died the death of a martyr. The following account covers the last two years in the life of this courageous young believer.

---

[1] One of the constituent republics of the USSR, lying between the Ukraine on the east and north and Rumania on the west; population 3,300,000, mostly of Rumanian extracion.
[2] A name adopted by the "unlicensed" (illegal) Baptists in the USSR, also called the "underground Christians" because they have no licensed meeting places and generally meet in secret.

CHAPTER 2

First Trials

The persecutions of Ivan Moiseyev began almost immediately after he was drafted into the Soviet Army. The following account of his first few months in basic training was taken from a tape recording which he made on furlough in May of 1972:

"When I first came to the regiment in Old Crimea[3], I began looking for a place to pray. I found a room which was empty until 10 a.m. An officer was working there during the daytime, but before he arrived in the morning no one was there. The soldiers were awakened at 6 a.m. every morning. I dressed and went to this room, where I stayed until breakfast. The soldiers were doing some construction work, but I myself prayed for two hours. Now and then I was late for breakfast because I didn't look at my watch.

"Two months went by like this. Then the day arrived when my faith in the Lord was to be tested. God showed me how I should act. On this particular morning I arose at 5 a.m. and prayed until nine. Just before nine I hurried to the morning roll call. Everyone was waiting for me, and they had all been looking for me. I had to explain my absence to the commanding officer. He already knew that I was a believer. The major ordered me to line up and said I would be punished. Our conversation continued on the training ground, while the soldiers were busy with war training. He tried to compel me to deny my faith.

"When we returned to the barracks I was summoned to the commanding officer. There my superiors talked with me. My punishment was that I should work all night. I worked with joy. I was to wash the floors in the barracks, and there were many of them. They had to be cleaned with soap and brush. I did it all and was happy. My superiors noticed this and then began

---

[3] The Crimean Peninsula, a near-island on the northern shore of the Black Sea, formerly an autonomous soviet, now part of the Ukrainian SSR.

calling me to one officer after another. Finally I was called to the highest officer, the commanding officer of the barracks. We talked for three hours.

"At first he was shouting, but he finally calmed down. I asked him, 'Do you mind if I tell you something?' He gave his permission, thinking that he had convinced me to deny Christ. But all the time I had been listening to the voice of God, not men. I said to him: 'Your shouting has been in vain. It doesn't scare me.' Then he took two chairs and offered to let me sit down. He wasn't so rude anymore, and finally when he realized that he couldn't persuade me he left.

"Then he sent me to another unit where I spoke all day with one of the higher officers."

"After 20 days and 300 miles of marching, we were finally sent to Kerch[4]."

---

[4] A port city in Eastern Crimea with a population of 114,000, lying on the Kerch Strait, a shallow channel separating the Black Sea from the Sea of Azov.

CHAPTER 3

Kerch

It was in Kerch that the persecutions of Ivan Moiseyev began in earnest. His refusal to disavow his faith had only stiffened the military's determination to break him. By December 1970 the pressure was on the increase, as his furlough tape relays:

"December 1970, the Old Crimea. Here they really started to take me in hand. At least 15 times each day I am called to various departments to be pressured.

"Once they asked me, 'Have you ever been sick?' I answered, 'No, I don't know even what a hospital is like.' They probably thought, after five days without food I would become ill, but I didn't. The first day passed like an ordinary day and so did the following days, thanks to God. I did not become ill, because I prayed all the time. They asked, 'Well, have you changed your opinion?' Finally I was taken to the X-ray department and declared to be healthy. Then they left me alone. Finally, all this came to the authorities' ears and they said, 'Give him something to eat, for if he dies from hunger we are in trouble.'

"One night I was forced to stand outside for five hours. The temperature was twenty degrees below zero and I was dressed in my summer uniform. They didn't see how I could possibly spend five hours out there. I prayed without ceasing. I didn't know what time limit they fixed — a whole night or one or two hours. After a while I was called in and asked, 'Have you changed your mind, or haven't you?' Then out into the cold again. But I didn't feel the cold. When the officers happened to come out for just 10 or 20 minutes they were shivering with cold. They looked at me and were astonished that I didn't freeze. Once I had to stand out for a whole night, then several nights in a row. This continued for two weeks. Then I was allowed to sleep in the barracks with the other soldiers.

"The first night after the trial in the cold they gave me per-

9

mission to sleep in the barracks after 10 p.m. I fell asleep and the soldiers were also sleeping. Suddenly an angel came to me and said, 'Ivan, arise.' I thought I was dreaming. I remember how I got up and dressed and flew away with the angel. We didn't fly through any door or window. The ceiling just opened up and we flew up in the air. 'You must follow me, because you don't know anyone here,' the angel said. I understood and followed.

"We crossed a big grassy field and arrived at a small river. The angel walked across the river, but I was afraid. He asked me, 'What are you afraid of?' 'Snakes,' I said. 'Don't be afraid, I am here. It is not like the earth; there are no snakes here.'

"I followed him and there the angel showed me the apostle John. He flew up to me and told me through the angel what it was like to be there. It was more light there than on earth during the daytime but I didn't see the sun anywhere. The next person the angel showed me was David the Psalmist. After David he showed me Moses and then the prophet Daniel. I didn't speak to them, but the angel spoke and told me afterwards.

"Then the angel said, 'We have walked a long way and you are tired.' So we sat down under a big tree. 'I wish to show you the heavenly city, the New Jerusalem,' the angel said. 'But if you see it as it is you can no longer live, and you still have much to do on earth. We'll fly to another place and I shall show you just the light from this city, so without dying you will know the New Jerusalem really exists.' When we arrived I saw high mountains. Between the mountains was a deep gorge. The angel took me down into the gorge and said, 'Nothing will happen. It's all right for you to look.' Then the angel said, 'Time has come to fly back to earth.' We flew back. I remember how the ceiling of the barracks opened and we descended slowly to the floor.

"The angel was standing at one side of the bed and I at the other. In the same instant I heard the officer on duty shouting, 'Everyone up!' The light was switched on and the angel disappeared. I noticed that the bed was made and that I stood fully dressed. I remembered everything the angel had shown me.

"My neighbor from Oleneshti, Suvorova District, Moldavian SSR, got up and asked me, 'Where have you been tonight?' I said 'Don't you remember how I undressed last night and went to bed at the same time you did?' He answered, 'Yes, it is true, we went to bed at the same time, but later you disappeared. Did you go to town? Come on, let's ask the officer on duty.' The officer assured us no one had been out during the night. 'I watched the door,' he said.

"Finally I told everyone about my journey with the angel, but they didn't believe me. For the next two days I had a strange feeling and wondered where I was living. The news about my adventure with the angel spread to all the barracks. At once my superiors began new attempts to persuade me. This time the pressure on Ivan Moiseyev escalated directly into physical torture. In January 1971 he was deported to Sverdlovsk[5], where, from the following short account, he was apparently turned over to local agents of the KGB[6], the Soviet secret police.

"In January 1971 after treatment in the military department I was put in a special car for prisoners and sent in the direction of Sverdlovsk.

"Here I was placed in solitary confinement and then transferred to five different cells for special torture. The first cell had a couch were I could lie down. The second cell was smaller. Here I could only stand up and sit on the couch. The third cell was a cold cell where I had to stand upright and icy water ran constantly from a shower in the ceiling. The fourth cell was the frost cell and all four walls had refrigeration installed.

"The fifth cell was the torture cell. Here I was dressed in a rubber suit which was pumped full of air so that it put great pressure on the body. This pressure was gradually increased. Now and then I was asked, 'Well, do you change your mind? Otherwise you will have to stay here for seven years.' I answered, 'If it is God's will, I shall stay here for seven years. If not, then you will have to stop your torture before tomorrow.' This lasted for 12 days, after which I was brought back to the city of Kerch."

---

[5] A large city, population 919,000, in the Russian Soviet Federated Socialist Republic (RSFSR), the largest Republic in the USSR; located about 1300 miles NW of the Black Sea.

[6] So-called 'Committee for State Security,' whose agents are noted for their sadistic inventiveness.

CHAPTER 4

The Fingerprints Of God

The next few months in the life of Ivan Moiseyev might, in the light of the cruel physical privations of the barracks and the overt torture of the KGB, be regarded as somewhat of a 'respite.' Although the psychological harassments continued unabated, the tortures had subsided — at least for a time. It was also a period when God revealed Himself, not only to Ivan, but also to his unbelieving military companions. The furlough tape continues:

"Often I was called into the staff. They spoke to me, questioned me and made threats — all with the one purpose of changing my opinion and making sure that I had no spare time. Ten times a day was not enough. Now and then I was called 15 and 20 times.

"One day our company gathered for a political discussion. At first only about 20 people were present. The officer who was to lead the discussions didn't show up, for some unknown reason. Then the soldiers decided to hold the meeting themselves and the topic they chose was: 'What is the difference between your God and ours?' They asked me, 'Who is your God?' I answered them, 'My God is Almighty.'

"A sergeant from Erevana in Armenia[7] said to me, 'Now if your God is almighty and if he lives and can do anything, then let him give me a leave of absence. Then I will believe in him.' All the soldiers nodded and said, 'Yes, if God can do this then we will know that God really exists. Sometimes we think that what you tell us are just fairy tales. Now if your God does *this* then we will believe that he is a living God and can do anything.' I prayed silently and the Lord revealed himself to me thusly, 'Tell him that I can do it.' Then I turned to the sergeant and said, 'Tomorrow you can go home on your leave, but first do what I tell you.'

---

[7] Armenian SSR, constituent republic bordering Turkey and Iran; population 2,164,000.

He was smoking. 'Drop your cigaret,' I said. He then threw it away. 'Now take the package out /of your pocket.' He took the whole package out and burned it.

"While this conversation was taking place the whole unit of 150 men was gathering. Then the officers came and sent us all back to work. In the evening I again met the sergeant and we talked the whole night through. We had only two hours' sleep. He promised me that he would believe. I gave him some advice on how he should act while traveling on leave and while staying at his home. His parents were not believers and knew nothing of God. So far, he had not even mentioned the leave to the officer on duty.

"In the morning, shortly after we had gotten up I was sent after some provisions in a military car. Afterwards, when I came back, someone told me that a very high military man, a general, had phoned from the regiment in Odessa[8] and ordered this sergeant home immediately. But I don't think it was the general calling; I think it was the angel. All the papers were quickly made ready by the staff and he went home on his leave.

"When the soldiers heard this, they told the officers what kind of 'political discussion' we had had. They also told that everything I had predicted had happened. Immediately the officers sent some soldiers off to stop the sergeant and bring him back, in order to change the opinion among the soldiers that Ivan's God had given the sergeant his leave. But it was too late. He had already taken the train and they couldn't get hold of him.

"I was immediately called in to talk with the staff. There the major-general, who was the division commander, was waiting. He asked me what had happened. I told him all about the 'political discussion' of the previous day. 'But how could you tell the sergeant was to go on leave?' he asked. I answered, 'God did it.'

"This general wanted to send me away to another unit. The staff considered his proposal, but the soldiers supported me. They all left their jobs and gathered outside the staff building to show their support. Therefore I stayed with my unit.

"There were some more political discussions and then we were sent to an uncultivated field to clear it. Sometime after we returned from the field, and the sergeant returned from his leave, the

---

[8] Major port city of the Ukraine, with a population of 735,000, located on the NW shore of the Black Sea.

regiment was summoned to a meeting. Here I was threatened and derided because of my prediction. They tried to ridicule the incident of the leave, but the sergeant himself stepped forward and said to them, 'What power could have done this? I believe God exists because when you denied me a leave God performed a miracle which was evident to all of us.' There was much excitement and enthusiasm among the soldiers, but the officers went away in shame.

"Sometime after this, in November 1971, I was to be sent to the city of Vostena in the Odessa District. They gave me a truck in order to go to the bus station at Zatishiye. On the way to the station the truck broke down at about 10 p.m. I crawled under the truck to see what had happened and decided to remove the drive shaft. I removed the shaft with a monkey wrench. When it fell off, I barely managed to dodge it. With the shaft off, the truck, being on a slope, started to roll forward, catching me on the shoulder and chest. The total weight of the truck was 14,000 pounds. There were two soldiers standing nearby. I shouted, 'Lift the back part!' The soldiers worked and sweated for ten minutes to get me free. At last I was free and stood up, but immediately fell to the ground, unconscious.

"I was taken to the hospital in Zatishiye, but not a single doctor was on duty. I noticed that I had frostbite and that my right arm was hanging down, lifeless. They rushed me to the city of Simferopol[9] and put me in a military hospital. They took me to the X-ray department. I was in for a complicated operation: amputation of my right arm and half of my lung! My temperature was 107.

"I prayed so loud that all the sick heard me. Then I fell asleep, absolutely exhausted and very feverish. When I woke up the next morning, I noticed that both of my arms were lying under my head. And my chest felt so good. I thought it was a dream. I fell back asleep again.

"When the doctor made his rounds he gave me a thermometer. I said, 'I don't have any temperature.' The doctor then gave me some medicine, saying 'Take this!' I answered, 'But the medicine doesn't help.' The doctor was frightened. He thought I had lost my mind. I said, 'I knew that you couldn't cure me, so I turned to my heavenly doctor. He cured me last night while I slept.'

---

[9] Large city on the Crimean Peninsula, population 213,000, about 120 miles W of Kerch.

The doctor was even more bewildered. I gave him the thermometer. It showed 99 degrees.

"They called me to the doctors' conference room. There were three doctors present. The local surgeon, a first lieutenant, asked me, 'What happened to you, Moiseyev?' I told him everything that happened, including my being healed by God. He said, 'You were to have your right arm amputated and half of your lung removed. For the first time in my life I see a miracle. Really, God does exist.'

"I was discharged at once. I had to go through a room where 200 soldiers and officers were lying. All were astonished to see me on my feet again; the word about me had spread. I went to the bus station. In the meantime, the chief surgeon of the Crimea was called in and arrived in a great hurry. The doctors told him what had happened. He didn't believe it and hurried to the bus station where he met me. I refused to go back, so he examined me with great astonishment and then left without a word.

"I arrived back at the unit in Kerch. All the soldiers had heard about the wondrous healing and were astonished to see me. But now the real trials began.

"It is true, as it is said, that when God reveals Himself, the devil gets very angry. So he was furious and ordered much evil to be done against me. I was often called to hearings of the staff and threatened.

"One time I was walking through the park, singing. It was a clear winter's day. Then I suddenly saw an angel descend from the sky, like a distant but very clear star. He came down right in front of me. I continued walking towards the staff building and he followed me, right above my head. Then the angel said, 'Ivan! Go on, don't be afraid, I'll be with you.' The angel followed me till I reached the building, then disappeared. I think he was in the room but I didn't see him, and the officers didn't see him either. Still I sensed the presence of God all the time, and I was not scared by the threats.

"Some time later, I was driving a truck fully loaded with bread. The bread was placed in special drawers. The back doors of the truck were locked by two bars and a padlock. The sergeant was with me in the truck. I suddenly heard a voice say, 'Slow down, Ivan.' I didn't really understand and went on. Once more I heard the voice but for some reason I didn't obey. I looked at the speedometer. Forty miles per hour. Suddenly I saw a loaf

15

of bread in front of the car, rolling along with the same speed as the car. I immediately understood this vision. God wanted me to stop.

"I stopped the truck and checked it, along with the sergeant. The door was locked and the padlocks still in place. We opened the door and were amazed to see that half of the loaves were gone. We looked back down the road and saw that they were lying scattered all over the road. The sergeant was astonished and said, 'Ivan, tell me, didn't we lock the doors together and very thoroughly? I have been driving this truck for six months and never has anything like this happened to me.' But I knew that God had stopped us. He knows what lies ahead. We gathered up all the loaves and started out again about 45 minutes later.

"I said to the sergeant, 'We will drive on.' But he asked me, 'Why did the loaves fall off?' We had not gone far — just to the first crossroad — when we saw that a great accident had happened. A bus which had overtaken us while we were collecting the loaves ran into a large crane. All on the bus were dead. We would have died there, too, if God had not stopped us. I thanked God, because He has said, 'I am your God and protector.'

"We came back to the regiment. The sergeant told everybody about the incident but no one believed him. I was called to the officers and the hearings started again. I explained, 'God saved our lives through the miracle with the loaves. He loves everybody and is ready to save everybody; you are also among them. He can save you from the eternal punishment which is in store for everyone who doesn't receive Jesus Christ."

Thus ends the testimony of the furlough tape of May 1972.

CHAPTER 5

Last Letters

The period shortly following the furlough tape appears to be the turning point in the persecutions of Ivan Vasilyevich Moiseyev. Up until that time, there seemed to be only sporadic and unsuccessful attempts to compel him to deny his faith, either by intimidation or physical torture. But shortly thereafter, as the following letters make clear, a definite conspiracy to kill him was hatched, a cold-blooded cabal which found its sadistic fulfillment on July 16, 1972.

It is probable that there were letters *before* the May 1972 tape as well, but the translator or those responsible for smuggling the documents out apparently felt that the tape covered the substance of the story adequately up to that time. Since in all probability the author did not return home thereafter and so would have had no further opportunity to tape his recollections, the letters after May 1972 would have been the only documentation available. Hence their inclusion by the translator, albeit in somewhat shortened form.

The letters themselves are eloquent testimony to the innermost thoughts of the writer. It is obvious, particularly in the last several letters, that he sensed the end coming, whether he had ostensible evidence of it or not. (According to a note by the translator, the unpublished sections of the letters make it clear that he was, on six or seven different occasions, given a deadline before which he must change his conviction; hence he must have known that his continuing refusals would sooner or later bring down full retribution upon him.) But the most remarkable thing the letters show is his composed and even cheerful reaction to the impending doom. There is, in his simple Russian prose, a transparent Christian love, a sense of total self-sacrifice and an almost Pauline manner of expression.

The first letter, dated June 3, betrays a deceptive calm before the storm:

June 3, 1972

"I greet you all with the great love of Jesus Christ. It is Ivan writing, the least of your brothers in Christ.

"I can write this letter in full freedom, since after the happy meeting with Sergei[10] there has been no trouble at all. I am certainly happy for it, but when there is no storm, no trials, everything seems so quiet. I am so used to trials.

"What a happiness, what wonderful joy there is far away from the earth. Brothers, I urge you always to go forward; don't be frightened even if you have to go through fire on your way to the heavenly goal. If your heart loves other things more than Jesus then you can't follow Him.

"Now I would like.to tell you what the angels' bodies are like. We shall have bodies like this, too, if we are faithful unto death. I asked if I could see the angels and I saw them. I saw how they are dressed, which I told you about. Their bodies are not like ours; they do not block your sight. You can see through them as through glass, and they are as pure as crystal both inside and outside. You can see everything inside. They do not have any sin, not even any faults. One day we shall have a spiritual body like this, too. When we have got such a body we will be able to see everything, even Jesus, the angels and the Father. Then we can know what they think, too. Oh, what a joy, what purity and love is there. Just think, everyone will be so pure. You can polish a piece of glass as much as you like, but it will still be dirty compared to these bodies.

"I will be waiting impatiently for your answer. I wish for you all that you may walk forward towards the land of heaven."

Ivan

Unknown date

"Peace be with you, my beloved parents. Some of my brothers in Christ from Zaporozhe[11] have been to visit me here. It was wonderful, even though some from the official Church have been reporting that I was preaching Christ.

"Though I am a soldier now, I still work for Christ despite trials and sufferings. Jesus Christ has given orders that the Word of Life must be proclaimed both in the city and at every meeting of soldiers and officers. I have been to the division staff and in

---

[10] Apparently, from later context, another Christian soldier on the base at Kerch.
[11] Large city, population 550,000, in S. Ukraine, on the Dniepr River.

the Special Department.[12] It was not easy, but the Lord saw to it that the Word was received even there, even among the highest in rank.

"Those who live not according to the will of man but according to the will of God shall be saved. Take heed of the commandments of Jesus.

"Later I shall tell of more wonders and revelations which I have had."

Ivan

His next letter disclosed the existence of a colony of believers in the town of Kerch and another city.

June 15, 1972

"Greetings in Christ, dear parents. I got your letter. It was a joy for me. I would like you to know that I am in good health by the great love and grace of God.

"When I was home Ilyusha[13] taught me a hymn. Ilyusha, keep on learning more hymns by heart. Teach the older people the hymns also so they can join in the singing. Yesterday I was in a meeting in Kerch and met the brothers in the congregation, which is not registered and is not a member of the Union[14]. There was a brother there from Sochi[15]. They had heard about me even there. It was so good to meet with each other. All the friends here including the one from Sochi send greeting to all the brothers in Moldavian SSR.

"The Lord has shown me the way and I must follow it. But I don't know if I will be forced to give up — the fight is harder than before. But I am not afraid. Jesus walks before me. So do not be grieved, dear parents. I love Jesus more than I love myself. I know His presence even if my body sometimes trembles and finds it hard to obey. I don't even value my own life as much as I value Him. I don't walk around with my own thoughts but only with the Lord's will. If he says go, I go.

Don't be sad if this is the last letter from your son. For when I have a revelation I hear the angels talking and I see — yes, I am astonished and find it hard to believe — that Ivan, your son, is

---

12 Department of the Soviet Army dealing with 'special' problems such as political deviation, subversion and espionage.

13 Probably the writer's sister.

14 Union of Registered Churches, i.e., those approved by the Soviet government.

15 Health resort city on the Black Sea in SE European RSFSR; population 179,000.

talking to the angels. I, Ivan, who was also a sinner and trangressor, but through the sufferings of the Lord I was cleansed of my sin. Now I no longer live as I want to, but according to the Lord's will.

"I also write to those who do not believe in our Lord Jesus so that they may know — even if they do not believe it — that there is a God, He who gave me life. And for you, Simon, my dear brother, so that you can know that the Heavenly Father will give you eternal life. Well, I am a little disappointed over you. Much has happened since last time and now I am far away from you. In order that you, too, Simon, might know that there is a God, I want you to know and believe that I have been speaking to the angels and have flown away with them out in the universe where an eternal life is waiting for us. May you also believe it, you who know nothing about the other life. I write you because I have seen it all."

Ivan

July 9, 1972

"I send you my greetings, but they will soon stop. I feel a little weak, but I greet you with the love of Jesus Christ and the peace of God. They have told me that I must not preach about Christ, but I answered that I could not stop witnessing about Jesus.

"It is not easy to be in this kind of service to the Lord; we know that. But I go to meetings now in spite of their forbidding me to do so. The brothers here send greetings to you all. I also send greetings to Slabodeyska and Jermokleya[16].

"I wish that Senya and Galya[17] would come to believe in the power of God and also experience it. I wish that they could clearly see that God exists as does everyone here. The superiors and the soldiers all talk about God's existence, and they are afraid, because they see wonders and God's power.

"I wish, too that Grandmother would come to believe and that she would understand that the path she is walking leads to perdition. Still Jesus Christ is calling and he will give eternal life. Believe in the gospel. If you should hear that I am no longer free, then I want you to know that I have left a little notebook here in Kerch in which I have written down the wonders. You can go there

---

[16]Small towns in Moldavian SSR near the writer's home town, where other members of the ECB apparently lived.
[17]Identities unknown; perhaps personal friends of the writer.

or the brothers can come to you. Be true Christians. Jesus gives you of His strength power. Ask, for He is rich in everything and whatever you desire He will give it to you freely. I do not forget you in my prayers. The Lord be with you."

Ivan

July 11, 1972

"I greet you all with the love of Jesus Christ. It is Ivan who is writing to you. I love you so much. You should know that they have denied me any form of leave. But I still work for Christ with full power. I will not boast of it, but I want you to know about it so you do not forget me in your prayers.

"On the evening of the tenth of this month I was preaching Jesus Christ and one soldier turned to Christ. I became so happy and was filled with such power. I give God the glory for everything. If we meet again I shall tell you all about it. I cannot write about it.

"Incidentally, I have a feeling you will not see me again.

"If you think of coming here to see me, I can say it will be of no use. I will not forget you in my prayer. Maybe my last task is nearly behind me. Receive this sincere greeting from the least of your Christian brothers. Greet everyone. I do not expect an answer; neither do I ask you to write.

"Goodby and the Lord be with you, dear friends. I am thinking that it is difficult for you, but remember that I go to carry out Christ's commandment."

Ivan

July 14, 1972

"The greetings from your son will soon cease. They have forbidden me to preach about Jesus Christ. They do not allow me any rest. I have many trials. I have told them I cannot stop talking about Jesus Christ. I am obeying the commandment of Jesus. Trials are great and the sufferings are not easy. I have much to tell but it is difficult in a letter. Everybody here sees the miracles and says, 'Truly, there is a God.' I will go forward as the Holy Spirit and the angels lead me. The superiors and the soldiers say, 'There is a God,' because they see the miracles and His power.

"It has been a heavy storm. I was promised that I could see Sergei, and now look forward each day to this. I shall tell you about it afterwards. Ahead of us now is a Christian battle, and I go into this battle with the commandment of Jesus. Sergei must be here when we begin this fight. We must show how a believer should act and live. We do not know what will happen but we have prepared for it long ago.

"I want to send you, my dear friends, young and old, a verse from Rev. 2:10:

'Do not fear what you are about to suffer. Behold,
the devil is about to cast some of you into prison,
that you may be tested . . . Be faithful unto death
and I will give you the crown of life.'

"Receive this greeting. Maybe it is the last one from your little brother Ivan."

Ivan

His last letter was written to his younger brother Volodya:
July 15, 1972

"Little brother, I have received your letter but have been delayed in answering because there has really been a storm here. They have found and confiscated postcards and literature from Sergei. Now don't go tell this to mother and father. Just tell them, 'Ivan has written a letter to me. He writes that he is following the commandment of Jesus Christ to go into Christian combat and he doesn't know if he will ever return'.

"Receive this greeting which may be the last here on earth from the least of your brothers."

Ivan

CHAPTER 6

Death Of A Martyr

From the documents that follow, it is apparent that on July 16, Ivan Moiseyev was arrested by his military superiors, perhaps in company with civilian agents of the KGB, severely tortured, and then finally drowned in the shallow channel of the Kerch Strait.

As with the other material comprising this account, the attempt has been made to preserve the simple, peculiarly Russian flavor of the translation, even at the expense of smoother literary quality.

The principal document, a semi-official report by 68 members of the so-called Council of Relatives of ECB Prisoners, provides the main body of details:

"While serving in the Soviet Army, Unit 61968-T, our son and brother Ivan Vasilyevich Moiseyev died on July 16, 1972 in the city of Kerch as the result of a horrifying and cruel torture because of his faith in God.

"Tortured and beaten, but still alive, he was drowned in the Black Sea in five feet of water, he himself being six feet tall. This happened under the supervision of first lieutenant V. I. Malsin. The certificate of death stated: '. . . caused by drowning' The autopsy analysis concluded: '. . . death caused by violence.'

"On July 17 we received a telegram, saying, 'Your son has died in a tragic way. Please notify us when you will arrive to claim the body.' We came to the city of Kerch and decided we would bury him in our own town. They showed us our son's face while lying in the coffin. Then the zinc coffin was riveted shut. We had come with our son Simon, who is a member of the Young Communist League. He was summoned into a special office where he spoke for a long time with the military superiors, but afterward he never mentioned a word of this to us.

"In order to be present at the burial and help with the transportation of the coffin back to Volontirovka, the captain of the military unit, V. V. Platonov, the commander-in-chief, and several soldiers from the unit came along. The coffin arrived in the city on July 20, 1972.

"When we got the coffin home we decided to examine our son's body and take some photographs. We began knocking off the nails riveted into the lid. At this point captain V. V. Platonov and the commander-in-chief became uneasy, saying, 'We must go now. We are in a hurry.' They got into their car and quickly drove away. When the coffin was open we started to take the clothes off the body to examine it, but suddenly our son Simon made great protests and tried to stop us by violence, saying, 'Take pictures of him with his clothes on.' But we nevertheless took a look at the body. Around his heart there were six deep stab wounds made by a sharp object; on both sides of his head were open wounds; his feet were marked by severe blows and on his chest were large burns. He also had blue marks at the corners of his mouth.

"In the testimony of V. I. Malsin from his talk with Ivan's relatives was the following statement: 'In the morning on July 16 I was busy speaking to a group of civilian guests. After noon I drove to the beach together with Moiseyev[18] in the car with the license tag GAZ-69.'

"But, according to some soldiers who were eye-witnesses, Malsin was driving the car with the tag PRAVDA, along with some unknown civilians[19] and Moiseyev was following alone in the car with the tag GAZ-69, toward some unknown goal. When Malsin returned to the barracks, he told some of the soldiers, 'The death of Moiseyev was hard. He fought with death, but he died as a Christian.'

"When the body of Ivan was handed over on July 19, 1972, Malsin was heard saying, 'This is the seventh pack of cigarettes I smoke today.' On the first of August 1. 1972 he was heard saying, 'My wife has lost 30 pounds in a week as a result of the incidents around the death of Moiseyev. Never again will I set foot in the car he was riding in.' "

(Signed)

The Council of Relatives of ECB Prisoners

* * *

---

[18] Ostensibly for swimming, since the weather was hot and the area suitable for bathing.
[19] Possibly KGB agent.

The second part of the 68-signature document of the Council of Relatives was the so-called

OPEN LETTER TO ALL GOD'S CHILDREN WHO CONSTITUTE THE CHURCH OF OUR LORD JESUS CHRIST:

"We were all filled with grief upon seeing Ivan's family around the coffin crying. They could hardly recognize the features of their son. We were unable to comfort them, but they found comfort in the fact that we all have a Father, the Comforter, who is also a righteous Judge.

"Many people were gathered at the funeral of the tortured and murdered brother; some who had come from a long distance as well as local brothers and sisters. Together they all had a devotional for the Lord.

"The funeral took place in the afternoon of July 20, 1972, amid hymns and Bible readings. There were many wreaths with Scripture verses in the Moldavian and Russian languages, such as:

"For me to live is Christ, and to die is gain."
"Do not fear those who kill the body but cannot kill the soul."

"The ungodly have been brought to light. Their wickedness has multiplied in the recent tragic death of our dear brother Ivan Vasilyevich Moiseyev.

"After having buried the body of our murdered brother Ivan we returned to our home with a holy desire to serve God yet more zealously — even unto death.

"Yes, even in our own day the 'extraordinary' has happened. Make this known to all nations who love the Lord, so that all who trust in the Lord and long to meet with Christ will turn to Him to defend and preserve the truth.

"Your brothers and sisters from the congregations of Slabodeyska, Benderska, Ermokleiska, and Tirapolska[20] present at the funeral on July 20, 1972 in Volontirovka."

(68 signatures)

---

[20] All towns in Moldavian SSR.

CHAPTER 7

An Appeal For Justice

In their desperate attempt to obtain justice, the parents and relatives of Ivan Moiseyev, apparently gave up early on trying to cope with the stubborn reticence of the local military unit at Kerch. In a move that seems startling in the totalitarian Soviet state, they sent their appeal for justice to the very top officials of the government, with copies directed to various notables both in and out of the USSR.

The documents display the lack of organization and polish one would expect from a Russian peasant family, as well as a poignant sense of frustration and futility, almost as if they knew that their efforts would be in vain:

A REPORT

TO: The Minister of the Armed Forces in the USSR,
A. A. Gretshko
The General Secretary of the Central Committee
of the Communist Party in the USSR,
L. I. Brezhnev

COPIES TO:
The General Secretary of the United Nations,
K. Waldheim
The International Committee for Human Rights
The President of the Academy of Science in the USSR,
M. B. Keldyish
The Chairman of the Council of Authors in the USSR
The Editors of *Sovietskava Rossiya, Pravda* and *Izvestiya.*
The ECB Church Council of the USSR
The Council of Relatives of ECB Prisoners in the USSR
All Concerned Christians

FROM: The family of Ivan Vasilyevich Moiseyev, tortured

and murdered for his faith while serving in the Soviet Army.

We, the parents of Ivan Vasilyevich Moiseyev, ask the following:

1. That a committee of medical experts be sent immediately to conduct an autopsy on the mutilated body of our son.
2. That an investigation be made to find the criminals who murdered our son.
3. That a group of believing Christian doctors be allowed to accompany the medical committee in its autopsy.
4. That we be given at least four days' notice of the arrival of the committee.

"We Christian parents still have four sons younger than Ivan who have not yet served in the army. As long as the murderers have not been found, the case not investigated and a reasonable assurance of the safety of our believing sons in the army not given, we will not send our four sons into such service.

"To this request we enclose the following:

1. Documents from witnesses
2. Copy of certificate of death
3. Photographs of the body will be handed over to the committee of experts when it arrives

Respectfully yours,
(Signed)
V. T. Moiseyev
I. K. Moiseyev
V. V. Moiseyev
P. V. Moiseyev
N. V. Moiseyev

Please reply to:
The city of Volontirovka
Suvorov District
Moldavian SSR

The document of the witness, cited in (1) above, reads as follows:

ENCLOSURE

"We, the undersigned, testify that the received body of Ivan

27

Vasilyevich Moiseyev, soldier serving in military unit 61968-T does not correspond to certificate of death #286064 IAP, stating, '. . . caused by drowning.' We certify this with photographs and facts: the heart is pierced six times, feet and head bear marks from heavy blows and burns on the chest."

Witnesses, citizens of Volontirovka, signing,

V. T. Moiseyev

I. K. Moiseyev

(a total of 23 signatures)

CHAPTER 8

A Letter To The World

The final document comprising the account of the death of Ivan Moiseyev was an open letter from the ECB Council of Relatives, dated August 1972. It apparently served as a 'cover letter' for the entire collection of documents smuggled out of the USSR and is addressed primarily to Christians in the free world:

"Dear brothers and sisters:

" 'Precious in the sight of the Lord is the death of His saints.' (Ps. 116:15). Even more precious to Him is the martyrdom of one who has faithfully witnessed about Christ.

"We have handed over extensive material about this young Christian man's martyrdom. It includes documents, photos, letters, tape recordings and eyewitness accounts.

"With great pain we pass on this terrifying example of injustice and capriciousness. It is a repetition of what happened to our brother Nikolai Chmara with the exception that it did not happen in the prison of Barnaul[21] but within the ranks of the Soviet Army.

"The information we pass on does not have the purpose of arousing indignation against those who persecute the Church of Christ in our country or those atheists who support them, but first of all to call them to repent, and that they may understand that they will inevitably be held responsible by the righteous Judge, who will demand from them an accounting of all the innocent blood which has been shed in our country and who will judge them according to their works.

"Secondly, the Council of Relatives of ECB Prisoners, together with the parents of Ivan Moiseyev wish and ask God that many children of God and all Christian young people, as a result of Ivan's martyrdom, might be filled with His Spirit for a more

---

21 City, population 382,000 in S central RSFSR, like Sverdlovsk, apparently a headquarters of the KGB.

self-sacrificing testimony that Jesus Christ is the Saviour and the answer to a world heading toward destruction.

"The coming of the Lord is near. He has been witnessing about this in revelation which brother Ivan received during his last days and also through many other brothers. The number of those who are to be murdered for the sake of God's Word must be completed. Therefore he had to walk this path. In this way the testimony which this faithful child of God made before his death had great power, not only because of the Holy Spirit but because of the blood this martyr shed.

"Certain facts about the well-planned murder of our brother Ivan are concealed from us. But to God nothing is covered that will not be revealed.

"We believe that God in the near future will reveal everything to us which can serve to glorify His name and save those souls who were witnesses to the murder of the young preacher Ivan Moiseyev. This is a basic law in the spiritual battle; the death of the first martyr, Stephen, had a harvest of a hundredfold for the Kingdom of God, because it aroused the persecutor Saul to a self-sacrificing service for Christ.

"As brother Ivan returned to his unit after his last visit home he agreed to have his picture taken. He then said, 'You can have this picture as a memory. I will never have an opportunity to see it myself.' Now he looks at us, this courageous Christian soldier, from a picture taken eight days before his death. Beside it is the picture of a dead body with the marks of the cruel torture he endured as his tormentors tried to tear out the heart that had unshakeable faith in Almighty God. But praise God, they did not succeed. The could only torment the body but could not damage the soul. He died for Christ.

"Jesus Christ was crucified and through his death he defeated the world and our persecutors.

"They can only be cleansed from their shame through tears of repentance and the blood of Christ.

"May the eyes and hearts of many Christians be opened to see this victory.

"May the Holy Spirit through this inspire many to great achievements for the Gospel."

    (signed)

Council of Relatives of ECB Prisoners

August 1972

CHAPTER 9

Epilogue

It would seem that the significance of the story of Ivan Vasilye-vich Moiseyev is severalfold.

To begin with the least significant, it shows the changing nature of modern Soviet society. In a time when political and intellectual dissent in the USSR is becoming more commonplace and out-spoken, it is significant that the present account indicates the exact same trend in religious matters as well. The numerous Christian congregations in the various towns, the outspokenness of the soldiers in their support of their ill-fated compatriot and the fact that the parents and the ECB Council of Relatives went directly to the top of the Soviet hierarchy in their protest—all this shows that an easing of religious suppression seems to be taking place right along with the general thaw, notwithstanding this brave martyr's cruel and arbitrary death.

It is also evident that God is moving in Soviet society as never before, as more and more Russian citizens join the body of Christ. God has apparently not found the Iron Curtain an insurmountable obstacle, notwithstanding the atheistic bravura of communist propaganda.

Of greater significance in this poignant drama is its highlighting effect upon the spiritual condition of the church in the free world.

While Christians in the Soviet Union and other communist countries bravely go to their deaths or face hideous tortures for the faith, their counterparts in the western world often shrink from speaking of Christ even in polite company for fear of ridicule or ostracism. While brothers in the scattered congregations of the Russian hinterland risk exposure to send their love and greetings to each other, their western friends spend much of their time haranguing and condemning each other over theological trivia. And while the simple Russian believers spread their faith in spontaneity and joy, their free-world cohorts often use neatly-

31

trimmed systems of "canned" evangelism to take the reality and involvement out of witnessing.

If anything, the story of Ivan Moiseyev should make those of us in the free world aware of the great responsibility we have to use our freedoms wisely to spread the Gospel, lest everything which we so blithely take for granted be taken from us.

But perhaps of greatest significance is what it shows about the life and person of one simple, committed believer. Little could be added to the testimony of the ECB Council of Relatives who wrote such an eloquent epitaph in their letter to the world. Perhaps we can turn only to the Word of God itself for an adequate description of this courageous young martyr:

". . . my faithful one, who was killed."

Rev. 2:13

If you are interested in further information about the Christians in the communist world, or wish to receive our bi-monthly news letter, please send us your request to Danish European Mission, Hoje Gladsaxe 36, 2860 Soborg, Denmark, Europe.